NEW ZEALAND IN COLOUR

VOLUME TWO

Beech tree, Lower Hollyford Valley

NEW ZEALAND

IN COLOUR—VOLUME TWO

PHOTOGRAPHS BY

KENNETH AND JEAN BIGWOOD

TEXT BY JOHN PASCOE

A. H. & A. W. REED

WELLINGTON · SYDNEY · LONDON

First published 1962
Reissued 1962, 1963, 1965, 1966, 1967
Revised edition 1969
Reprinted 1971, 1972

A. H. & A. W. REED LTD

182 Wakefield Street, Wellington
51 Whiting Street, Artarmon, Sydney
111 Southampton Row, London, WC1
also
29 Dacre Street, Auckland
165 Cashel Street, Christchurch

© A. H. & A. W. REED LTD

ISBN 0 589 00470 0

KYODO PRINTING COMPANY LTD., TOKYO, JAPAN

INTRODUCTION

AWARENESS of landscape and seascape should come easily to New Zealanders looking at these pages. Many of the scenes will be evocative of their travels and experiences. Overseas readers will find comparisons and contrasts with their own countries. The eye of the beholder finds beauty where it will.

There is more in photographs than the expression of composition, more than clouds or weather, more than beauty; studies of landscape in their own right have so many aspects that the rewards are not limited. Brilliance of colour may be effective, for nature herself can be brilliant. Remember also that nature can be delicate, as in the pastel shades of winter, and vigorous, as in the rebirth of spring sunlight. Photographs of scenes we know are nostalgic to the memory; those that we have not known before are enticing for the future. It is a matter of mood, and of responding to a mood.

New Zealanders may be charged with making their myth of country as with making their myth of man against the elements, the bush, and the mountains. But this is not a book of philosophic speculation as much as an offering of realities. Does the landscape and the climate affect national character in the way that Spain affects Spaniards or Norway affects Norwegians? Other books will resolve such problems and explain why Westland produces West Coasters and the Waikato gains dairy farmers. The validity of our awareness is perhaps dependent on the critical facility with which we answer it. What do we value in our scenery? Is progress synonymous with dross and harm? If we can respond to scenery with such questions, the replies are not material; scenery has made us think, and that itself is valuable.

Photographers who can master the difficulties of colour processes have this in common with writers, artists, and musicians: their creative feeling is that of the interpreter, who expounds theme, story, form—call it what you will. History and topography are relevant to landscape photographs. A scene of pasture, river, lake, or mountain gives the key to many things. It may be to a story of human endeavour, if not of human occupation; to work, sports, relaxation and travel. It gives too the key to the relation of one feature to another; the fascination of knowing that the snows of that mountain feed that river, and thence, that lake, and again thence, another river and perhaps a hydroelectric power scheme.

Thus the sight of Mount Cook from the Hooker Valley in Canterbury can mean many things to many people. The overseas visitor can wonder at the majesty of the mountain. The artist can puzzle over the colours of a changing sky and find flecks of shadow in rock. The botanist can contemplate the Spaniard plant in the foreground and the hunter wish to shoot chamois and thar. The naturalist can seek sight of the birds that live in forest, scrub, and rock. The kea is a clown for everyman.

The skier can pine for the upper snows of the Tasman Glacier, out of sight but not out of mind. The mountaineer can reflect that in the eighties Edward Whymper, pioneer of the famous Matterhorn, was nearly invited to attempt the then-virgin Mount Cook. He can admire the young New Zealanders who in 1894 made the first ascent, and used the Hooker approach, and he can agree with the regret of one of these men who wrote after his climb "there is but one Aorangi". The Maori scholar can debate the time-honoured question whether Aorangi means "cloud in the sky" or "sky piercer", or was named for the youngest in the party of Maoris who discovered it. And many can recall that New Zealand's most famous mountaineer, Sir Edmund Hillary, left his mark on Mount Cook when in 1948 he took part in a new route to the low peak by way of the great south ridge.

Thus the photograph on the back of the dust jacket of this book, which speaks especially of human courage and natural beauty, has these qualities reflected in a scene of complete contrast on the jacket front. Oruaiti Beach at Waihau Bay, in the far east of the Bay of Plenty, was once called Whangaparaoa by the Maoris. Tradition records, that, centuries ago, canoes of the "Great Fleet" made landfall here after the long voyage that began near Tahiti. Legends link the flowering pohutukawa trees with the arrival of the canoes, pohutukawas that the New Zealand poet Allen Curnow has described as "woody tumours burst in scarlet spray".

There is no need to labour the point. Full captions to the pictures give information for those who wish to know more of their story. New Zealanders, Maori and Pakeha, are shown in these pages by implication only. The book speaks for the land, touched or untouched by man; it is left to other books to speak for and of the people.

If this book gives particular stimulus it will be to travel throughout New Zealand. What do North Islanders, or South Islanders, know of New Zealand, who only the North Island, or the South Island know? That stimulus to travel has not been the aim of the photographers and publishers; rather it has been to give a better knowledge of New Zealand to their fellows, as to readers beyond the Tasman and Pacific. But it is satisfying to think that those who contemplate the views in print may be impelled to see them in person.

For myself I have been privileged to introduce, and I have tried to do so calmly, country that I love with fire and passion; and provide details that are not always implicit in the pictures. Let no more be said; it is for you to browse, to reflect, and to consider.

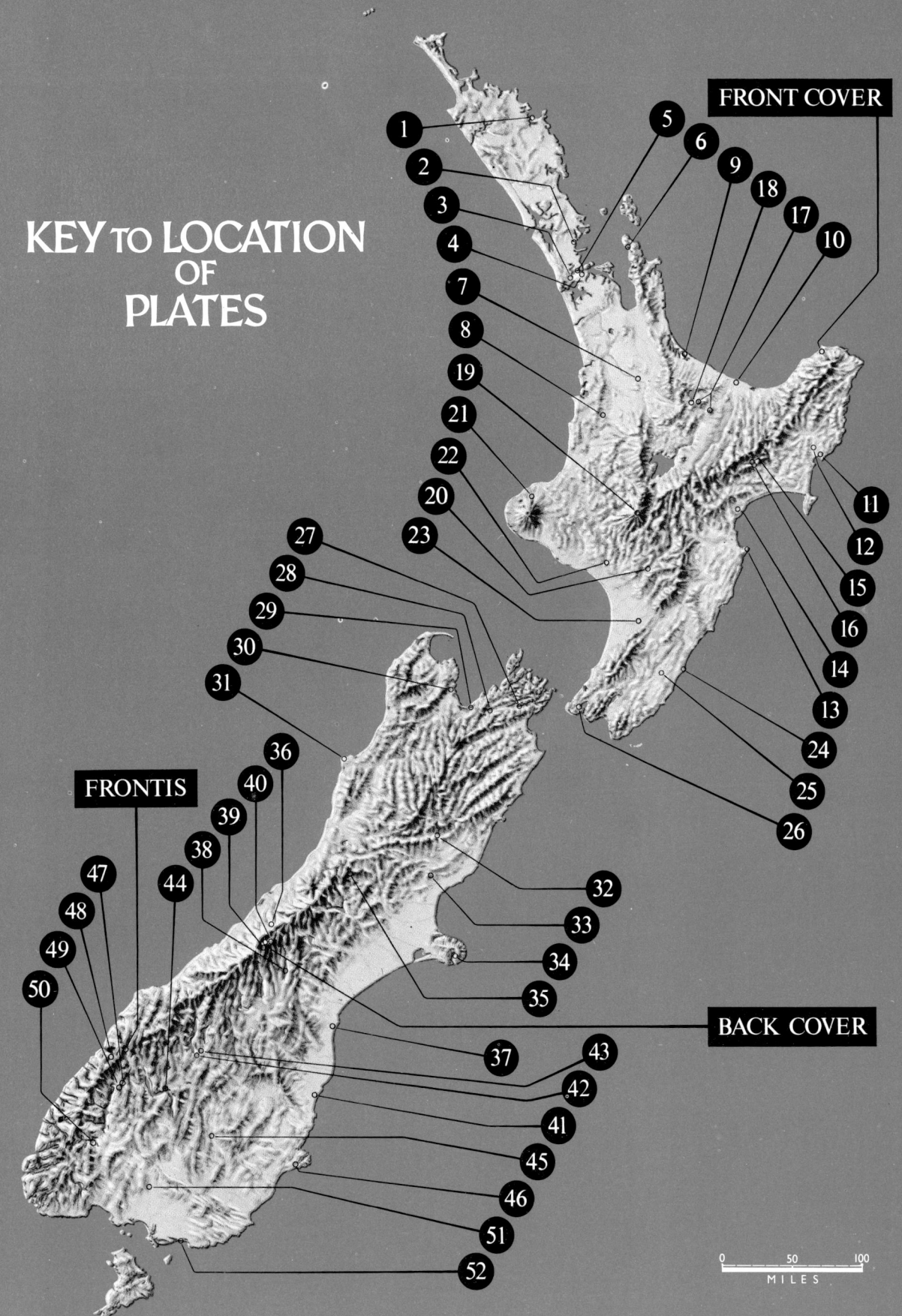

KEY to LOCATION OF PLATES

FRONT COVER

FRONTIS

BACK COVER

0   50   100
MILES

NEW ZEALAND is a little country of great contrasts. Her history, as her scenery, probes the imagination. Here is an example: this quiet and peaceful holiday settlement of the nineteen-sixties was once the thieves' kitchen of the far north, the wildest port in the South Pacific. It was a long haul from Sydney or Hobart, still longer from New Bedford, London, or Le Havre; as companions the whaling men had ex-convicts from New South Wales and impressionable Maoris.

Consider the canna lilies in the foreground, the family at the slipway on the left, the sightseers on the wharf, and the trees vying for space with comfortable houses. Consider Hone Heke, who in 1845 cut down the flagstaff on the hill behind this viewpoint. In those days Russell was Kororareka; it was sacked and burnt; some of its defenders died and were buried in the churchyard half-hidden by the boughs of the pohutukawa whose shadow embraces the beach.

Let your eye follow the wharf to halfway; raise it to the dignified house whose roof is silhouetted by bush. That is Pompallier House, home of Bishop Pompallier, pioneer Roman Catholic missionary of early New Zealand. The original building had mud walls, believed to have been built in 1842. Today Pompallier House is preserved as a historic place, visited by countless New Zealanders and overseas visitors.

One of the launches at the wharf proclaims its vocation by the raked outriggers for the big-game rods. The gathering of onlookers suggests that a party is about to leave for Dog Rock and Piercy Island, and suggests also that it will be a little while before the larger passenger launch sets off to explore the bay and some of its 150 islands.

PLATE 1
Russell township, Bay of Islands, Northland.

WAIWERA is literally "the place of hot waters". Thermal springs by rivers and lakes inland are known to many New Zealanders, but there are only a few places where they are found in the sand of sea beaches. The springs of Waiwera on a coast of the Hauraki Gulf were known to Maoris, whose method of bathing was to dig a large hole in the sandy beach, and to sit and talk in the hole when it had filled with hot water. In those days the bay was protected by four fortified pas.

A pioneer's reminiscences record that at one time 3,000 Maoris were seen on the beach. In his early days, the only way of reaching Waiwera was by sea. A boat would land passengers, who were met by a horse and dray, and thus ferried ashore dryshod. For well over a hundred years the curative value of the springs has been known to Europeans. Today a modern hotel is the hub of the bay.

At this point thirty miles north of Auckland the main highway to Northland gives a sparkling view to the Whangaparaoa Peninsula, narrow and graceful under clouds—themselves forming a peninsula in a sea of blue sky.

It is a great charm of this bay that it has not yet been overwhelmed by too many houses. The bush, the swimming, and the beach can be enjoyed by those who cherish peace in a relative sense. Whether you pass through Waiwera by car, visit it by launch or yacht, or fly over it in a small aircraft, the bay is one of the most impressive in a part of New Zealand that abounds in good beaches.

PLATE 2

Waiwera River and Beach, north of Auckland.

THE Tasman Sea rolls in on Bethells Beach and Piha, just over the skyline, but the Waitakere Range chops the westerly winds down to size before they reach this green valley of the grapes. The Waitemata Harbour is equally close, less than ten miles away, but its breezes are relatively mild.

The vines green-stripe the sun-baked soil of the valley floor and line its gentler slopes, springing powerfully from the rich earth, and the grapes—Palomino, Chasselas, Pinot, Cabernet, Malbec, Muscat, and Gamay—ripen to firm sweetness in the trapped sunshine.

Most Henderson vineyards are tended by New Zealanders whose grandparents and great-grandparents learned to cultivate soil for grapes in Lebanon or Syria. The Mount Lebanon vineyard, for instance, was founded sixty years ago and named for one in the Mediterranean homeland.

Half-an-hour distant by road, Auckland city rushes about its business, and if time does not actually stand still in Henderson Valley at least it moves at its own fair pace, unrationed and unregulated by the parking meter, the traffic light, and the office clock.

PLATE 3
Vineyards, Henderson Valley, near Auckland.

"FOUR white tents and a few scattered raupo huts, scarce visible amidst the tangled wood around, containing about sixty individuals...One solitary barque then lay at anchor in the harbour...The suburbs were a brown waste..."

This description of the early eighteen-forties from an official's journal compares well with his notes of the change wrought by a further six years. "The smoke was curling upwards from the roofs of the numerous farm houses around, giving cheering evidence of the residences of industry...carts were passing to and fro, and bands of natives were hurrying on droves of pigs...now it [the plain] was covered with cultivation, settlers were busy at their various occupations and its surface was sprinkled with sheep and cattle..."

What of Auckland of the nineteen-seventies? Each reader can find his answer in this view from the War Memorial Museum in the Auckland Domain. Part of the city is so clear that Aucklanders will be busy identifying buildings in the photograph. The brown hill on the far side of the Waitemata Harbour entrance (right centre) is North Head; behind it the landmark of Rangitoto, symmetrical extinct volcano, protects the harbour from storms in the Hauraki Gulf.

If Auckland were a person, it would be known as a character in its own right. Auckland is wealthy, commercial, industrial. Auckland has crowds, yachting, garden suburbs, traffic congestion, large stores and tall buildings, sports grounds, parks, and a complexity of local bodies. It is very much aware of its existence and of its significance for lesser cities. It has many voices within its gates and one voice for the rest of New Zealand. Its Parliamentary seats are the key to political power; its influences on art, music, and literature are also considerable. Auckland has truculence, peace, humidity, clarity, New Zealanders, foreigners, ferries, buses: thus could the list of opposites continue. Yes...Auckland is a city of character, for characters, and though Auckland does not often glance to the south, New Zealand will often contemplate the north.

PLATE 4
Auckland and the Waitemata Harbour.

THE isthmus between the Manukau and Waitemata Harbours is crammed tight with fifty, sprawling, jigsaw suburbs. Across a mile of salt water lies the North Shore, where there is still ample room for the city to grow, and where a ten-mile chain of beaches provides a more relaxed way of suburban life. Harbour ferries took thousands to work and back again, but the motor roads around the harbour were long and the vehicular ferries inadequate for the vast increase of traffic.

Aucklanders decided they needed a harbour bridge. They faced the practical realities of engineering and finance and by 1959 their problems were resolved; the harbour bridge was completed. For once statistics are as vivid as adjectives. Four million pounds were spent for the bridge of 3,348 feet in length. Weights of steel total 7,035 tons, and concrete and roading 6,680 tons. The centre arch is 146 feet above the water and has a span of 800 feet. Eight lanes of traffic take a bridge gradient of one in twenty.

The bridge exemplifies beauty of design as well as metropolitan pride. As night falls the lights of the bridge and traffic send their signals of achievement. This view from London Street on the Ponsonby (southern) side of the harbour is a tribute to Auckland foresight as to Auckland growth. This bridge was widened in 1969 but Aucklanders are already talking of yet another Harbour Bridge.

PLATE 5
Nightfall on the Auckland Harbour Bridge.

FORTY miles north of Coromandel the road ends in this bay, a place of holiday camp sites, fish, and history. It is close to Cape Colville, named by Captain James Cook in 1769 after the lord and admiral under whom he had served in Newfoundland.

The view tells of intricate reefs leading towards Square Top Island, and, far beyond, of Great Barrier, the largest offshore island of the north. As with sunlit mountain scenes, this calm day does not hint at the hidden fury of the skies, nor tell of the high seas and scouring rains that can sweep the Hauraki Gulf. Indeed Great Barrier Island has a sad record of shipwrecks on its coast; in 1894 the S.S. *Wairarapa* and 121 lives were lost.

The two green-topped tents tell of campers who give their days to swimming, fishing, and boating. Think of the calm dawns, the resolute sunshine, and the night dew on surrounding grass. And Colville Channel leading to the open sea. Think too of the Maori inhabitants of the past, their first contact with European navigators, and the wealth of Maori history that lies in the soil of bays such as this, awaiting the trowel of the archaeologist and the radio-carbon dating of the scientist to find and establish in time their age-old *pa* sites.

PLATE 6
The bush-lined road between Whitianga and Kuaotunu, on the Coromandel Peninsula.

EXILES from villages in Cambridgeshire were reminded of their homes as English trees flourished in new settlements on the banks of the Waikato. Today the town of Cambridge stands as a permanent record of the nostalgia of those pioneers.

Drive up the Waikato valley towards Tirau, and you will find the lake formed by the Karapiro hydro-electric power scheme. The dam is one of a series designed to exploit the full resources of the Waikato River from its birth in the snows of Ruapehu to its magnificent storage in Lake Taupo and its subsequent descent to the sea. The length of the Waikato at two hundred and twenty miles has a variety of bush and farm land as well as power realised and power potential.

The relatively new lake of Karapiro is ideal for aquatic sports and regattas. In such peaceful surroundings it is salutary to remember that European settlement in the Waikato included land confiscated by the Government from the so-called rebel Maoris, further that armed constabulary built the first road from Cambridge to Tirau.

The Waikato Valley is vulnerable to flooding in its lower reaches and a special authority was formed to cope with its problems. The intensive dairy farming of the Waikato has laid fields and hedgerows across its plains and low hills, a pattern of prosperity as well as of pastoral calm.

PLATE 7
Lake Karapiro on the Waikato River.

NIGHT above the earth has beauties, mysteries and exaltations, dangers and sorrows for mankind. Night below the earth is eternal.

Men who explore deep and continuous caves face difficult problems; their discoveries are seldom shared by their fellows. The Waitomo Caves, explored in 1887, are an exception. Since they were made accessible for tourists they have brought to their recesses many people who would never have travelled to the hilly pasture lands between Otorohanga and the reaches of Kawhia Harbour on the west coast of the North Island.

The Maoris used the name Waitomo, meaning "water entering the hole". In fact a Maori guided Fred Mace, sailor and survey assistant, when he first followed the underground stream on a flax-stick raft through the lowest level of this complex cavern.

The Glow-worm Grotto has the fascination of myriad specks of light—the luminescence of a hundred thousand insect larvae, the grotesquerie of jutting rock, the solemnity of height, and a calm passage of water for its boatload of visitors. One New Year's Eve, Queen Elizabeth and the Duke of Edinburgh included this sight in their New Zealand tour.

PLATE 8

The Glow-worm Grotto of the Waitomo Caves.

EXOTIC forests and paper pulp account for the increased importance of Tauranga Harbour. Here the S. S. *Alaric* passes pleasure launches moored beside Mount Maunganui, its eastern head.

J. C. Bidwill, botanist, wrote of Mount Maunganui in 1839 that it was "a curious hill, or immense rock of basaltic lava mixed in some places with pumice . . . formerly a very strong 'Pa' (Pah), a native fort or village" and that it was a "splendid object; were it necessary it might be made a second Gibraltar". Although Mount Maunganui, the "large mountain" of the Maoris, is sacred to them, as to local historians and admirers of unspoilt symmetry, there is a proposal to build a night club on the top, 762 feet, to be served by an aerial ropeway and car. Such is progress!

Tauranga itself is Maori for "sheltered anchorage" or "resting place for canoes". It has a fascinating history. The mission station was founded in 1835 and the mission house, "The Elms", was built in 1847. "The Elms" is one of the most historic houses in New Zealand and much of its present furniture dates from the pioneering period of Archdeacon A. N. Brown. There are other places of historic interest in Tauranga, such as the Gate Pa, scene of a Maori-Pakeha battle in 1864, the mission cemetery, and the Monmouth Redoubt.

Tauranga has expanded rapidly in recent years. Its climate and situation make it fashionable as a holiday resort and a desirable place for retired businessmen and farmers; it is close to deep-sea fishing, serves a prosperous farming country and is accessible by road, sea, railway, and air. Tauranga beaches are crowded, its harbour alive with small craft and there are many camping places.

PLATE 9
Tauranga Harbour and Mount Maunganui.

"A GREAT river like a full tide" is one version of the Maori name of this river, ninety-five miles in length. A soldier in the Maori Wars described the Rangitaiki thus "... leaving the Taupo plateau [it] flows eastwards through the Kaingaroa plains, as sterile and desert as those it has quitted, washes the foot of the mountains forming the northern boundary of the Uriwera [Urewera], near Mount Edgecumbe [Edgecumbe] pours through a narrow defile, and lower down unites its waters to those of the Tarawera river, both falling into the sea at Matata, under the name of Te Awa o te Atua (the river of the Spirit)." Though the reference to the Tarawera River is inaccurate, the quotation makes the point that the upper reaches of the Rangitaiki were once in "sterile" country.

Today this country is clothed by the Kaingaroa Forest, one of the greatest man-made forests in the world, source of timber for the mills of pulp and paper at Kawerau, where a new town and a new industry have been built at the foot of Mount Edgecumbe, shown to the left of this photograph. This extinct volcano, nearly 3,000 feet high, is a landmark of the Bay of Plenty and was named by Captain James Cook after his sergeant of marines.

This reach of the Rangitaiki River is at Thornton, north-west of Whakatane, close to the coast. Reflections of trees and sky; promise of good trout fishing; these add to the attractions of this corner of New Zealand.

PLATE 10
The Rangitaiki River near Whakatane, Bay of Plenty.

WHEN in October 1769 Captain James Cook made his first landing in New Zealand it was on a beach at the foot of Kaiti Hill. Because the large bay "afforded us no one thing we wanted" Cook named it Poverty. Polynesian voyagers had been more fortunate there and had found fertile land for settlement.

Their descendants named the site of Gisborne "Turanganui," the stopping place of a famous voyaging canoe, and for some years of European settlement this Maori name persisted. In March 1868 two tribes sold 741 acres, the nucleus of Gisborne, for £2,000. In 1870 the first business sites were sold and the highest figure was recorded at £51 for a section of a quarter of an acre.

Gisborne was named after a Colonial Secretary of the 1860s. It served a growing farming community and its freezing works depended on sea for transport, until in 1943 the through railway from Napier was completed. Today good roads and a nearby airport supplement the harbour and make light of former inaccessibility.

The climate here is one of the best in New Zealand. The hill country is well stocked, and the lowland produces citrus and other fruit. Motorists find Gisborne the entry point of magnificent tours, whether around the East Coast past the spectacular bays of Tolaga, Tokomaru, and Hicks, or through to the Bay of Plenty by the more direct gorge route of the Waioeka.

This lookout from Kaiti Hill shows distant spurs and buildings crosslit by a late afternoon sun. It looks indeed a promised land. Gisborne thrives on its sunshine, as on its farming products, and in summer the offices close early to allow its population to swim at the beaches with which it is generously endowed. Needless to say, people rise for work early in Gisborne.

PLATE 11
Gisborne from Kaiti Hill.

THIS carved meeting-house at the foot of the Kaiti Hill, Gisborne, typifies the Maori *marae* (community centre and village green) as found throughout the North Island. On these *marae* ceremonial and tribal occasions take place and visiting groups are welcomed with speeches, action songs, and dances. The canoe *poi*, here photographed, combines song and graceful movement to tell of a canoe party paddling downriver. Traditional costume, too, is graceful and blends well with the intricate carving and colourful rafter patterns of the meeting-house.

The performers in the foreground are members of the Waihirere Maori Club. Normally you would find them working on farms or in offices, hospitals, shops, restaurants, or post offices. Maori clubs are valuable to the Pakeha as well as to their own members. They keep alive Maori traditions and culture with a sincerity that, so far from being a mere concession to tourist interests, is a vital part of Maori life.

The drift of young Maoris from the country to cities takes them away from the advice and example of tribal elders. This in turn makes them restless for entertainment and for the company of their fellow people. The clubs give them something of the security that they left behind, and, with the practice of skilled games and dances, the young people hold to their pride of ancestry.

Unfortunately the Maori language is not taught in New Zealand State schools, and if it is easy to learn Pakeha ways this is often at the expense of Maori ways. New Zealanders, and today we include both Pakeha and Maori in this description, realise that as time goes on Maori culture is changing as European culture has changed over the centuries. There is a responsibility on both races to keep what they can of the Maori capacity for community co-operation, music, agility and grace inherent in their *haka* (posture dance) and action songs. And Maori oratory too has a pith and fluency that many a public speaker must envy.

PLATE 12
The Poho-o-Rawiri Meeting-House, Gisborne.

WHEN the great fish that is now the North Island of New Zealand was hauled from the sea by Maui, hero-god of Maori legend, he left his magic fish-hook embedded in the promontory now known as Cape Kidnappers. The Maoris called the place Matau-a-Maui, the fish-hook of Maui, but it is the name given by Captain James Cook for a much less significant event—the attempted kidnapping of a Tahitian boy from the *Endeavour* in 1769—that has persisted.

Cape Kidnappers forms the southernmost point of Hawke Bay, which sweeps to the north and east in a great sickle-curve, one hundred miles long. Nearby are the twin cities of Napier and Hastings, spurred on by keen rivalry, and a few miles to the south of the cape are the remains of the Rangaiika whaling station.

Today the cape is remembered by countless visitors to the gannet sanctuary, who have walked, tide permitting, along the beach from Clifton, five and a half miles away, and by a narrow track up the steep cliff above the cape. At the lighthouse plateau, 360 feet above the sea, there is a colony of nesting gannets, where the birds can be observed at close quarters. Another larger nesting-place is on the basin between peaks of the cape and there is a third colony on the Black Reef.

In 1880 the Cape Kidnappers colony had only fifty birds; now ten thousand populate the place. Whether gliding free on the up-draughted air, diving vertically for food into a shoal of fishes, courting, quarrelling, nesting, or feeding young, the gannet (Maori *takapu*) is fascinating to observe. New Zealanders are fortunate that these striking, confident birds, who most frequently live on inaccessible offshore islands, have made Cape Kidnappers their mainland home.

PLATE 13
The Gannet Sanctuary at Cape Kidnappers.

A GLIMPSE of lake and pasture land; a harmony of native and exotic trees; these mark Lake Tutira, a wild-life refuge on the highway from Napier to Wairoa.

In a young country such as New Zealand the names of outstanding pioneers are inseparably linked with the land they developed. "Tutira" means more than a lake to New Zealanders; it is perhaps the most famous of North Island sheep runs, for a fine book, *Tutira*, was subtitled by its author, H. Guthrie-Smith, "The Story of a New Zealand Sheep Station". The book is wide in its scope: natural history, ecology, pioneer farming, Maori lore, and philosophy.

Guthrie-Smith took up Tutira when it was an abandoned run, broke it in successfully with the energy of a young man and the vision of an older one. A keen ornithologist and a writer of several books, he studied soil erosion, climate, stock, and mankind with the same discernment, and left behind him wisdom for future generations. Here is a quotation from his last work, *The Changing Land*:

"Within a hundred years of New Zealand history has the home of the pioneer been changed from untilled bareness to garden and green trees, been beautified by sorrow, joy, and toil. Simple or gentle such a home has been a nucleus of culture and continuity, a centre radiating the ancient virtues of hardihood and simplicity. The pioneer himself, stubborn to endure, strong to subdue, heroic to defy, has passed away. The day has come to him, as come it must to all, when time has sapped the sinews of youth and bowed the strength that could not tire. Over the home paddock to the House of God nearby the slow procession of his funeral moved. Along the pilgrim's path that every man must pass has he been borne. The verdict of the world on work and worth, what left undone, what done, has been pronounced. 'His bones are dust, his tools are rust, his soul is with the saints we trust.'"

PLATE 14
Lake Tutira, Hawke's Bay.

STRONGHOLD of the Tuhoe tribe, the Urewera Country has a watershed more complex than any other in the North Island. Its main mountains are the densely-wooded Huiarau Range, named for an extinct native bird, which shelters Lake Waikaremoana, the Maori inland "Sea of Rippling Waters".

The first Europeans to see Lake Waikaremoana were Father Claude Baty, a Roman Catholic priest, and William Colenso of the Church Missionary Society, who arrived within a few hours of each other one December day in 1841. The Tuhoe Maoris were surprised in more ways than one by their unexpected visitors; a violent storm on the lake was accompanied by a four-hour storm of religious controversy between the two rivals.

Colenso's account of the lake is a vivid one. He described it as "very deep and clear, and the bottom rocky", and wrote "I was often struck with the magnificence of the waves ... altogether unlike in grandeur and high broken commotion to anything I had ever observed in those of the sea or ocean ... The continual noise by day and night caused by the winds and the waves dashing against the high rocky romantically-piled crags was deafening; all speech was with difficulty heard". Subsequently Colenso made other inland journeys, notably across the Ruahine Range, which established him as a botanical collector and explorer.

Here the clearing mists of the morning emphasise the scarred height of Panekiri Bluff, as seen from the grounds of the Lake House Hotel in the eastern arm of the lake; the bluff rises almost 1,000 feet above the lake. The Wairoa-Rotorua road follows the lake shore for fifteen impressive miles and gives ready access to this wild and romantic scenery, whose preservation is assured by the Urewera National Park.

PLATE 15
Lake Waikaremoana in the Urewera National Park.

THE dual leap of the Aniwaniwa Falls is framed to perfection by bush. The pool between them is foreshortened as though shy of showing its clarity; the rocks jut boldly.

The falls are near the lake shore and easily reached from the highway, which crosses the Aniwaniwa River only a short distance from Lake House. Upstream on the same river and reached by a side road are the Papakorito Falls, also well worth a visit.

An easy hour's walk from the Aniwaniwa Falls leads along a densely-forested track to Waikareiti, a miniature lake whose calm waters hold seven small islands, on one of which there is yet another lake, with a hidden sparkle of amber water.

PLATE 16

Aniwaniwa Falls, Lake Waikaremoana.

"THIS is the most awful moment of my life. I cannot tell when I may be called upon the meet my God. I am thankful that I find his strength sufficient for me. We are under heavy falls of volcano—", Edwin Bainbridge, a young English tourist, wrote this at the outbreak of the Tarawera eruption in June 1886 and died shortly afterwards.

The serenity of our view from Lake Okareka has overtones of holidays and peace. Bracken fern and scrub have grown over much of the country where ash-showers fell on the land. You can see the crater-gap between the peaks of Tarawera, 3,646 feet, and the scarred gulleys on the steeper slopes, but the scene does not look actively thermal.

It is difficult today to envisage the eruption that split the mountain in two and made a rift some eight miles long. Twenty new craters belched forth their destruction, covered irretrievably the Pink and White Terraces of Lake Rotomahana, till then star tourist attractions, and buried three Maori villages.

Eye-witness accounts and surveyors' reports were grim with details of earthquake shocks, loud detonations, fireballs, an immense cloud of ashes, and dust which "quenched the bright moonlight and darkened the sky for hours after daylight should have appeared". Four thousand square miles were affected; fine pumice and volcanic ash covered a steamer far away in the Bay of Plenty.

It is a relief to turn to the present and contemplate the good fishing lake, the colourful outpost of suburbia on the peninsula, and the return of forest to the scenic reserve that surrounds most of the shore. Lake Tarawera itself is out of sight, immediately over the ridge that crosses the picture.

PLATE 17
Mount Tarawera from Lake Okareka, near Rotorua.

THE thermal region of Rotorua has history as pervasive as scenic wonder. Sometimes, as here, names give the clues.

Whakarewarewa is a war dance to make a show of force before the attack; in this case an uprising at Wahiao. Maggie Papakura records the name of an Arawa woman, Margaret Papakura, who at the turn of the century was a famous guide at Whakarewarewa, one who had rejoiced in Maori lore and legend, and who subsequently studied for a degree at Oxford and wrote a book, published posthumously.

The swirl of steam from the geyser highlights the swirl of thermal water passing its barrier of rocks. Dr John Johnson, New Zealand's first colonial-surgeon, gave a description in 1846 that could well apply to this scene. He wrote of "the volumes of vapour ascending and rolling around in every direction" and of "a clear mountain river ...gliding swiftly along between deep banks". And visitors to Whakarewarewa today will agree with this statement: "We were obliged to use great caution in traversing the ground, for fear of treading on some portion of the crust weaker than the rest, and thus being subjected to severe scalding, or burning."

There are other places of interest at Whakarewarewa, such as a model fortified Maori village and a large Maori school. Beyond the Maori settlement there are vast plantations of exotic trees planted and milled by the New Zealand Forest Service as part of a self-sufficient economy.

PLATE 18

Maggie Papakura Geyser, Whakarewarewa, Rotorua.

A STORM has cleared and the clouds are dispersing northwards. The purple of flowering heaths, the light green of flax, and the dark green of beech set off the expanse of mountain tussocks, and early winter snows leave their first powder on the volcanic scoria of Mount Ruapehu.

Ruapehu may once have been a more symmetrical mountain than it is today but countless eruptions have blotted out all but its most recent volcanic history. In this photograph the summit, known as Tahurangi, 9,175 feet, is out of sight because of the clouds and because its neighbour Paretetaitonga, on the right skyline, is from this angle dominant. Te Heu Heu, on the left, is another of the peaks, three of them over nine thousand feet, that mark the mountain. It is difficult for a stranger to realise that what appears to be a summit ridge emerging from cloud is in fact the edge of a plateau, in the centre of which is set a crater lake, sometimes erupting steam and ash, more often warm-watered and calm.

The view looking south-south-east is taken a few miles from the Chateau, a luxury hotel. Although many people travel to the Tongariro National Park for special interests such as tramping, mountaineering, botanical work, and the study of volcanos, by far the greatest number are sightseers in summer and skiers in winter.

The largest area of shadow on the mountain marks both the Pinnacle Ridge and the area where most of the chalets, lodges, and huts congregate. To the right of that shadow there is a diagonal valley, down which the clouds have sent a tongue. That is the line of the chairlift up the Whakapapa Glacier and the route of mechanical transport that takes tourists to a view at 8,500 feet of the crater lake. In winter time there are thousands of skiers on the mountain; waiting in queues for the chairlift or ski-tows, turning on steep slopes in dazzling runs, or sitting out a storm in their sophisticated mountain houses.

Ski-ing in the North Island has its focus on Ruapehu. A negotiable road, mechanical aids, a team of instructors, a spreading rash of lodges; these all contribute to a remarkable transition from a *tapu* mountain to a key playground for New Zealanders of today.

PLATE 19
Mount Ruapehu, Tongariro National Park.

BECAUSE rivers, falling steeply from ranges to the sea, are so significant in the geography of New Zealand, their names are often given to their surrounding countryside and gain more general usage than county or electoral names. Thus the Rangitikei River of our picture has also named the land it drains, a hundred miles of river valleys from the central plateau to the sea.

Here the river has left the high, narrow gorges, and is entering the lower valley between Mangaweka and Hunterville. Grassland, the home paddock, the homestead, vehicles and men at work, country road, river flat and hills of pasture, with the river winding beside papa cliffs—these are standard features of the Rangitikei district. Totaras and exotics alike cast shadows. It is near enough to noon and clouds gather behind the undulating range.

Of such a scene, one pioneer wrote: "The kowhai, in spring, glistens in the sun on the thousand and one flats on either side, and the myriad of tuis sent forth their joyful song, the stream of water sinuous, but confined in a narrow channel."

The passage of time has brought a main highway and a main trunk railway to the Rangitikei, now familiar to thousands of travellers on these routes from Wellington to Auckland and vice versa. The Makohine railway viaduct is near here, in a side valley between Ohingaiti and Mangaweka. For the most part the highway and the railway are cheek by jowl, and the river close by, till they part company north of Taihape.

PLATE 20
The Rangitikei River near Ohingaiti.

THIS dominant but extinct volcano is to the people of Taranaki what Fujiyama is to the Japanese.

Although it may be less frequently climbed than its noble counterpart, Taranaki people are well satisfied to have it in their daily lives; cradle of storms that nourish their rich pastures; symbol of noble symmetry of outline; focal point in any scenic view.

Abel Janszoon Tasman did not see the mountain in December 1642, but he named its neighbouring cape after a Batavian councillor, Pieter Boreels. Succeeding navigators were more fortunate: in 1770 Captain James Cook named the mountain Egmont after a First Lord of the Admiralty, John Perceval, the Earl of Egmont, and a year later the ill-fated Marion du Fresne sighted it and called it Mascarin Peak.

Since Mount Egmont was first climbed in 1839 by a German naturalist, Dr Ernst Dieffenbach, and a seaman-whaler, James Heberley, it has been the Mecca of many mountaineers, trampers and skiers. The approaches to Mount Egmont are good; metal roads and well-kept foot-tracks, hostels, huts, and bridges do credit to its National Park. The bush is spectacular with tall timber and ferns, and, near the scrubline, the trees stunted by storms and wind have grotesque forms and mossy festoons that talk of goblins and fairies to those who have read Irish folk tales.

It is ironic that Egmont, the mountain of invigorating ice slopes in winter and the scene of mass climbs in summer, the ideal training-ground for skiers and climbers, has the highest death roll of any in New Zealand. Thirty people have died on Mount Egmont. Accessibility has brought dangerous slopes close to those who take them too lightly. The view is halfway between Inglewood and New Plymouth. Eucalypts and pines claim most of the lake shore but the distant slopes of the mountain are, in the words of Dr Leonard Cockayne, "a magnificent natural museum of the wonderful New Zealand rain forest in the most perfect condition". To the south a sea of cloud contrasts with the satellite points of the Pouakai Range to the north. Mount Egmont is in a mood of serenity and the bellbirds sing.

THE tint of poplar leaves and the blue distant ranges,
The remnants of forest and echoes of warfare,
The settlers, the stock, the houses and farms,
Are part of river—the Wanganui story.

The gentle banks of the river below Pipiriki are in contrast to the cliffs of the gorge further up the valley. Its broad sweep resembles nothing so much as a swinging highway, and such a route the river was before the first tracks began to wind upstream from Wanganui town. Even so, the little steamers that replaced the dugout canoes and winched their way up the rapids or slithered back downstream served river settlers and tourists until some thirty years ago.

This view is characteristic of the North Island hill country. Today a good road to Raetihi leaves the Wanganui River at Pipiriki. Today men farm steep pastures; aircraft caress the slopes with fertiliser; some men even shear their sheep more frequently than once a year; and an uneasy balance is contrived between nature, whose advancing seedlings would revert the land to bush, and man who would clear it still further.

A prophecy of the forties by the traveller W. Tyrone Power—"the scenery as one ascends the Wanganui River is exceedingly grand and imposing, winding among precipitous mountains with small slopes here and there, which are taken up by native Pas and cultivations; every piece of available ground is thus occupied, so that there is nothing to tempt the settler in this direction"—has thus evaporated in the clear light of reality.

The valley is historic for Maori as for Pakeha. At Moutoa Island, well above this viewpoint, Hauhau warriors descended the river to attack Wanganui in May 1864; Wanganui Maoris defeated them.

PLATE 22
The Wanganui River from the road to Pipiriki.

TRIAL crops of the Grasslands Division of the Department of Scientific and Industrial Research at Massey University make an attractive pattern. Beyond the distant belts of exotic trees, the city of Palmerston North stretches itself to remind us that since it was first settled in 1870 it has grown to a population of over forty thousand people.

The wealthy farm lands of the lower Rangitikei and Manawatu are served by Palmerston North. It is a railway junction for lines to Taranaki and Hawke's Bay, as well as an important stop on the main trunk line to Auckland. Appropriately Massey University has a singularly important role in New Zealand's farming economy.

In its beginning in 1927 as Massey College, is was named for a farming Prime Minister of New Zealand. It then had the status of a university college of agriculture but it is now an autonomous body with the full name of Massey University of Manawatu. The original Act of Parliament defined the purpose of Massey College as being to advance knowledge in agricultural science, food technology, and related fields, and to spread that knowledge by teaching and research.

A scientific approach to farming methods and problems has given New Zealand a lead in many fields, and Massey University, with assistance from the Department of Scientific and Industrial Research, can rightly claim its share of credit for achievements and for planning for the future. The Dairy Research Institute is also situated at Massey University, although not part of the Massey organisation.

Nowadays Massey continues its agricultural role but has added other faculties, in the arts and sciences, to become an all-round provincial university.

PLATE 23
Experimental plots, Massey University, Palmerston North.

S WEEPING bays and rocky headlands mark the east coast of the Wairarapa at Castlepoint. The light-house stands clear on the left; beyond the rocky rib to its right there is hidden a shelf favoured by fishermen. Castlepoint is a popular holiday place for Wairarapa people who seek bathing and sunshine.

Castlepoint features in the pioneer travels in 1843 of William Colenso of the Church Missionary Society. He suffered gale and storm in the *Columbine*, a graceful little mission schooner, and when, weak from sickness after fif-teen days, he was landed at Castlepoint, he named its harbour "Deliverance Cove". Two years later, on his first complete coastal walk from Hawke's Bay to Wellington, Colenso revisited Castlepoint. His biographers, A. G. Bagnall and G. C. Petersen, have described the climb to "the sandy ridge above and beyond the white beach of De-liverance Cove, which ridge ran out from the mainland to sweep up steeply in a crested curve overlooking the pre-cipitous sea-worn eastern face of the Castle. From the ridge, 'a place of signal mercy to us on our first visit', the view of their future path was a twenty mile sweep of con-cave surf-footed hill faces softening down to the horizon of Flat Point, a lizard tongue on the morning sea."

This view looks north past white breakers to the blue horizon of the South Pacific. What tales could Castle-point tell of centuries of Maori settlement, of generations of peace, and cruel episodes of tribal war?

PLATE 24
Castlepoint on the Wairarapa Coast.

THE New Zealand Company chose the Wairarapa in 1845 as the site of a Church of England settlement, but the Maoris refused to sell their lands. By 1847 there were fifteen sheep or cattle stations, whose squatters leased their grazing land from the Maori owners at a total rent of £325, and whose stock totalled 73 horses, 1,365 cattle and 13,011 sheep.

Today there is a vast difference: although Maori land has an important place, there are also innumerable small freehold farms as well as larger runs. The small farms association founded towns such as Masterton and Greytown. They flourished; good roads and a railway made them relatively close to Wellington Harbour, and a railway tunnel through the Rimutaka Range has completed their accessibility.

The roads in the Wairarapa are not all highways. Some of the side roads that succour the more isolated parts of the coast rise and fall over very hilly country. Others, such as this one east of Masterton, at Tauweru, traverse pleasant pastoral valleys as well as ridges. Nearby the Mangapakia Pinnacles give an unusual break in the skyline, and beckon the traveller towards Castlepoint, shown in the preceding plate. Stock graze on good feed, well-painted farm houses are sheltered by clusters of trees, and most of the mustering can be done on horseback. Aerial topdressing has increased the fertility of the spurs and valleys.

The southern Wairarapa is known for its extensive lake of the same name, translated from the Maori as "glistening waters". There is a proposal for the reclamation of a large part of the lake, and if this work proceeds, some people will hope that marginal scrub and water will be left as shelter for the varied waterfowl that have for centuries populated it.

PLATE 25

A green valley in the Wairarapa.

I N her poem "Sunset," Eileen Duggan wrote of the city
and of the range of hills in the background...

    Low over Tinakori
    The west drops on the town
    What if on Tinakori
    The blazing sky fell down!

Night has now engulfed Wellington, which has retaliated with the sophistication of twentieth-century man. Yet even gaudy lights are softened by the harmony of harbour and sky.

Maori legend is rich in references to Mount Victoria. The oldest Maori name was Matairangi meaning "look-out post on a hill", and this was not inappropriate for British settlers who established on the summit a signal station for shipping. A later Maori name was Tangi-te-keo meaning "the sound of a bird's screech", referring to the taniwha (monster) that, failing to break out of Wellington Harbour through Kilbirnie Isthmus, flew in the form of a bird to the top of Mount Victoria.

The height of the summit is 648 feet, and it was named after Queen Victoria. In the seventies a gun was hauled to the ridge by the military and a charge fired daily to signal noon. The mountain is also the site of a survey trig station, a roofed lookout, and direction-finder. A new sweep of the scenic drive gives access to the striking panorama of city and harbour and a memorial to Admiral Byrd reminds visitors of American adventures in New Zealand's sector of the Antarctic continent.

Wellingtonians will recognise many features in this view, such as Oriental Bay (bottom right), a portion of the boat harbour, the Clyde Quay Overseas Passenger Terminal. On the right the radio masts identify Tinakori Hills, and the waterfront lights take their reflections to the harbour itself.

PLATE 26
Wellington by night, from Mount Victoria.

WHEN on 31 January 1770 Captain James Cook named Queen Charlotte Sound after the wife of King George III he drank her health in a good bottle of wine. The empty bottle was given to an old Maori who confirmed Cook's conjecture "about the Strait or Passage into the Eastern sea". As Cook's journey of discovery moved from the North Island to the South, so also does ours.

Becks Bay in the foreground in one of the many bays and coves invaded by the sea in this drowned valley of the Marlborough Sounds. Alas its bush slopes are anything but characteristic. Settlers' fires ran riot more in Queen Charlotte Sound than in her neighbour Pelorus, and although some of the hills carry stock, much of the country is poor and scrub-ridden, at the mercy of alien migrants such as gorse and natives such as tauhinu.

A scenic reserve guards this bay, which is served by a good road from the key settlements of Picton and Havelock, both named after British generals; the first killed at Waterloo and the second of Indian Mutiny fame. Such coastal roads give access to holiday houses and camps, and to safe anchorages for launches. The bush flanks include magnificent ponga ferns, whose spirals and patterns gave inspiration to Maori woodcarvers.

The Auckland poet, A.R.D. Fairburn, wrote well of the ponga in his "Conversation in the Bush".

> 'Observe the young and tender frond
> of this punga: shaped and curved
> like the scroll of a fiddle: fit instrument
> to play archaic tunes.'
>
>   'I see
>
> the shape of a coiled spring.'

PLATE 27
A bay of Queen Charlotte Sound.

PELORUS Sound is nourished by the tidal sea and fed by long reaches of the Pelorus River. Gaunt ranges of rock and mountain tussocks slope down to tangled beech forest where the young Pelorus gradually grows to a deep river. Few men know the headwaters at close quarters, but on some flights to Nelson, aircraft will give passengers a view of an amazing complexity of spurs and ridges affecting the river course with all the caprice of bluffs and gorges.

When the Pelorus River reaches the main highway bridge on the road from Blenheim to Nelson it has entered a stately scenic reserve of tall timber, motor camp and picnic grounds. Immediately downstream it is flanked by farmland, masked in this view by tall poplars. Only in winter has the water the tang of snow.

The sound and the river were named by Lieutenant Chetwode, acting commander of H.M. brig *Pelorus* in 1838 who, with whaler John Guard as pilot, explored the long series of inlets both for shelter and for curiosity. A provincial historian has thus described the exploit: "For eight days the brig sailed through the magnificent maze of mountains and hills. When the water shoaled the pinnace was manned and the river itself was explored to its tidal limits." Did the sailors strike a day as tranquil as this, when they passed these rocks?

The Maoris called the river Hoiere and tales are told that the peaceful reserve at Pelorus, where today children play hide-and-seek, cowboys-and-Indians, was the refuge of a fragmented tribe, hounded southwards by Te Rauparaha, "the Maori Napoleon".

PLATE 28
Winter on the Pelorus River.

EUCALYPTS and other exotic trees and shrubs border gardens in Nelson's suburb of Britannia Heights. The panorama is wide to the west and sweeps from the tableland of Mount Arthur to Separation Point.

Haulashore Island lies to the left; above, and very far in the delicacy of distance is Separation Point, the meeting place of Tasman Bay and Golden Bay. The Boulder Bank is a natural breakwater that made and preserved Nelson Haven for its discoverers. The harbour entrance has sometimes a current of seven knots with a tidal rise as high as twelve feet.

Maoris once used Te Whakatu, as they called Nelson, as a summer fishing ground. When Captain Arthur Wakefield, leader of a New Zealand Company expedition, was considering Kaiteriteri, on the other side of Tasman Bay, as a site for settlement, he learned of Te Whakatu. This prompted him to send a party to investigate. A bronze plaque on the Nelson foreshore erected by the New Zealand Historic Places Trust tells the story with precision:

CAPTAIN F G MOORE, D BROWN
J S CROSS MCDONALD AND PITO
HAVING DISCOVERED NELSON HAVEN
LANDED HERE ON 20 OCTOBER 1841

Moore's own account was "I walked to the top of the Boulder Bank ... and, to my surprise ... I saw a sheet of water considerable in extent, and to all appearances a good harbour".

For all its good harbour, climate, and urban population of 28,200, Nelson is unique in that it is the only New Zealand seashore city that has neither railway, nor regular ferry from other ports. For transport it depends on small coastal vessels, road services, and a fine airport. As it is the bottleneck for farming industries and for tourists, the air traffic is considerable. It has hopes, so far frustrated, of the establishment of major secondary industries.

PLATE 29
Nelson Haven and Tasman Bay from Britannia Heights, Nelson.

RIWAKA was examined for settlement in 1841. Within four years there were fifty people living in thirty-eight houses. Times in those days were hard. A pioneer remembered that the New Zealand Company had not kept the promise of two years' work. His people had only potatoes to eat morning, noon, and night. He wrote: "Mother made me a suit of clothes, trousers and all, out of a three bushel sack, and many others were dressed in the same manner."

The growing of hops was established before that of tobacco. Commercial tobacco-growing on a practical scale did not begin before 1916, but by the late twenties Riwaka, Motueka, and other Nelson districts were producing good crops. The latest figures show that the value of tobacco produced is over a million and a half pounds, and, with the advent of machine-harvested crops, reduced planting is offset by higher yields.

Hops too are profitable. Between 1,200 pounds and 1,500 pounds of hops are grown on each of the six hundred acres in Nelson Province.

Today Riwaka must be one of the most intensively cultivated districts in New Zealand. Raspberries and other fruit are lucrative for farmers, and with hops and tobacco attract seasonal labour from both islands. The community is as colourful as the environment and as sunburnt.

PLATE 30
Fields of hops and tobacco, Riwaka, Nelson Province.

ROCKY CORNER (*Clyppygen hoeck*) was the name that Abel Janszoon Tasman gave on 15 December 1642. Cape Foulwind was the name that Captain James Cook gave on 20 March 1770.

For once the open sea described by Tasman as "rolling …in huge billows and swells" and Cook as "a prodigious swell rolling in upon the Shore" is quiet, and low tide on the beach has revealed little rocky spines crosslit by the westering sun. Every rock glistens, and aloof in the distance rise the mountains inland from the Karamea Bight.

Here, where the sea has met the land in temporary harmony, on a coastline notorious for violent rages of wind and weather, is country made historic by the strivings of unknown sailors and by known explorers.

The view to the north recalls that Kehu, Maori guide to Thomas Brunner and Charles Heaphy in 1846, told them of the wreck of a three-masted vessel along this coast. As a boy Kehu had seen the bones of white men on the beach, and had been told that two survivors had struggled overland through the bush to Totaranui, below Separation Point, to be killed by tribesmen of the Ngati-Tumatakokiri.

The view also recalls the subsequent exploration by Kehu and Brunner, whose journey of 550 days included brave discoveries, protracted hardships, and near-starvation. Brunner's diary of 1847 tells of seals near Cape Foulwind, of sealers killing Maoris, of mussels among the rocks, of small potato gardens. Perhaps the most vivid entry was: "Rain continuing, dietary shorter, strength decreasing, spirits failing, prospects fearful."

Not far to the east of Cape Foulwind is Westport, at the mouth of the Buller River, a town whose fortunes were founded on gold and sustained by coal. The right angle of the cape protects the port from the worst of southerly weather, but the river bar presents a problem for even experienced pilots.

PLATE 31
Low tide at Cape Foulwind, West Coast.

RIVER beaches and rapids, blue pools and tawny ranges, wide flats above the river are familiar sights in the back-country of Canterbury. The scene is the sheltered Hanmer Basin, dry, sparse, sheep country where extremes of heat and cold mark the seasons. As elsewhere in Canterbury, the names of the Hanmer sheepruns—Woodbank, Rogerson, St James, St Helens, The Hossack, and Leslie Hills—are part of back-country history and geography. The river's original name was Waiau-uha, a "female river", who, according to Maori legend, wept for her mate, the Waiau-toa (now the Clarence) from whom she had parted. The Clarence has its source in the Spenser Mountains only a mile from that of the Waiau, but at this viewpoint is far beyond the distant range on the skyline. When these rivers enter the sea they are some fifty miles apart.

Mount Captain, 5,849 feet, is on the skyline, and was named for a horse that took its rider to the summit. Below lie the Hanmer Plains, first explored by runholders such as J. S. Caverhill and route-finders such as the Captains E. H. Dashwood and W. M. Mitchell, who were in 1850 determined to make a trail over which stock could be driven from Marlborough to Canterbury, where new flocks of sheep were urgently needed.

The hot springs at Hanmer were known to the Maoris and were found for Europeans by William Jones in April 1859. Today Hanmer is a popular resort for holidays, a forestry centre, and the site of a hospital for the treatment of nervous disorders. The transalpine highway from Christchurch to Westport follows the Waiau River and its tributaries over the Lewis Pass to the bushed gorges and river flats of the Maruia and Buller Valleys.

PLATE 32
The Waiau River near Hanmer.

NORTH CANTERBURY has a history inseparably linked with that of pastoralists. In November 1855 the settler who gave his name to Hanmer followed a rough road for station drays over the Weka Pass, doubtless the line of today's highway.

Limestone downlands and weathered outcrops mark the Weka Pass. The name weka was given by Maoris to the native woodhen; the bird may once have abounded near the district but today its habitat is far distant.

Beyond the pass lie the country township of Waikari and the Hurunui River. Further north again is the Waiau, and between the rivers is The Amuri, properly the Amuri Plains, a fertile farming region formed by the addition of centuries of wind-blown silt to gravel brought down from the eroding mountains behind.

Near the pass are caves containing Maori rock paintings of unknown age. One cave sixty-six feet long had eighty figures, each between two and three feet high. The carved names of visitors and heedless damage of stock rubbing the wall have spoiled many of the paintings, and further deterioration followed clumsy attempts at restoration. Fortunately other Maori rock paintings, in South Canterbury and Otago, are being preserved and recorded by the combined efforts of the Canterbury Museum, the New Zealand Historic Places Trust, and sympathetic landowners.

PLATE 33

A limestone outcrop above the highway near the Weka Pass.

AKAROA shares with Lyttelton Harbour the features of a volcanic crater filled by the sea. The Maori name, in South Island dialect, means long harbour. This distant view shows some few remnants of bush reminiscent of the lines by Mary Ursula Bethell who wrote in "The Long Harbour":

Grass springs sweet where once thick forest
gripped vales by fire and axe freed to pasturage;

It would take a book to give the full history of Akaroa; as yet that book has not been written. Although Captain James Cook sailed some ten miles south of Akaroa Harbour and named Banks Peninsula as Banks Island he did not attempt to land. South Pacific whalers knew Akaroa in 1835 and two years later a detailed American chart of the harbour was available in England.

Whaleships from France as well as from Australia and America appeared; one was in charge of Captain Jean Langlois of the *Cachalot*, who in 1838 bought land from the Maori and thus stimulated a French attempt to colonise Akaroa. That this attempt failed because the French did not gain sovereignty is another story, contested in the telling, but French settlers remained and their names with their descendants.

Lady Charlotte Godley wrote home in 1851 that "at Akaroa, we all at once found summer; for some days, it was so hot that we could not attempt to walk until quite the evening, and there are delightful walks in every direction ... the place seemed to me very foreign, from the people about being mostly French."

Today summer visitors still go to Akaroa, the harbour traps the heat and walkers explore the little town and the hills behind; and although the French blood has mingled with the British, its piquancy remains.

PLATE 34
Akaroa township and harbour.

Only a transalpine railway links Canterbury and Westland when the roads over the Main Divide are eroded by floods or blocked by winter snows. This view north from a terrace of the township shows the youth hostel, interdenominational chapel, and homes and cottages flanking the road to Westland as it heads north. In the distance power pylons march over the pass.

A ridge of Mount Rolleston rises on the left, and Mount Cassidy is on the right, above the cleft of the Devils Punchbowl Creek, whose falls are hidden from this angle.

On the extreme right, above the Bealey Riverbed, is the Canterbury entrance to the Otira railway tunnel, five and a quarter miles long. The Bealey Valley has beech forest characteristic of Canterbury ranges, but in Westland, on the Otira side, the rain forest is luxuriant. The main highway beyond the pass is steep and spectacular as it descends and traverses the Otira Gorge.

This is a summer view, a valley view, a restricted view. In winter the snows lie deep even on the river flats, and high above in the Temple and other basins, skiers swoop to sudden turns. Mount Rolleston, 7,453 feet, is the highest peak nearby; it has glaciers, five major ridges, magnificent rock and snow climbing, and offers traverses to the Waimakariri.

Arthur's Pass was nearly discovered by Samuel Butler, author of *Erewhon*, in his search for sheep country, but it was left for Sir Arthur Dudley Dobson to follow Maori information and cross in 1864 the pass that now bears his name. The gold rushes of the eighteen-sixties hastened the formation of a pack track and coach road.

Arthur's Pass is now the centre of a flourishing national park, whose boundaries enclose 239,152 acres. The railway and the road combine to bring many people to Arthur's Pass and the township has grown accordingly. Irrespective of the delights of ski-ing and mountaineering there are many other pursuits in this centre, which provides families with opportunities for holidays in the valley and on the mountains.

PLATE 35
Arthur's Pass and its township.

THIS is the "large land, uplifted high" of the journal of Abel Janszoon Tasman, navigator of unknown seas. It is fitting that his name rears proudly on New Zealand's finest ice peak.

The view from the Clearwater River is but a few miles from the Tasman Sea whose storms sheath the mountains with generous glaciers breaking to icefalls of impetuous proportions. These peaks are among the highest of the Main Divide of the Southern Alps, the ten thousanders. From left to right they are: Glacier Peak, Douglas Peak, Mount Haidinger, Mount Haast, and, to the right of centre, Mount Tasman, 11,475 feet. The icefall of the Fox Glacier is in shadow. Grassline and rain forest clothe the hills, part of the South Westland National Park.

In 1868 the geologist Sir Julius von Haast named the glacier the Prince Alfred and his book has this wry note: "... a few years afterwards, this glacier was visited by the Hon. W. Fox and re-named by members of his party, the Fox Glacier." But New Zealanders considered that as explorer and as Premier, Sir William Fox deserved the honour; and moreover Haast had tried to monopolise the naming of features.

With its neighbouring glacier, the Franz Josef, the Fox shares a glorious mountaineering history, whose great names include the guide Alex Graham, Canon H. E. Newton, and Dr E. Teichelmann. They carried heavy packs and made precarious high camps above the snowfields, braved storms, and climbed peaks. Today light aircraft shorten their routes, land gently in the snow and offload less hardy men in the heart of the mountains.

PLATE 36
The Fox Glacier and Mount Tasman, Westland.

HERE in South Canterbury is a wheat crop to recall verse by F. H. Woods:

When autumn comes with countenance so cheerful,
And offers man the riches of the land,
When fields of waving wheat turn richly golden,
We know the time of harvest is at hand.

And those of us who live out in the country
See that which many thoughtful folk adore—
The seas of wheat o'er which the wind-made wavelets
Sweep on and break upon a phantom shore.

Another New Zealander, Eileen Duggan, wrote in "The Farming Nation" about a working farmer:

He and weather have a meaning for each other
In a city, rain lies barren in a street,
But a farmer's rain is married to his paddocks,
And a farmer's sun is mid-wife to his wheat.

Wheat has a long history in New Zealand. The first missionaries taught Hongi, the great leader of the Nga-Puhi in Northland, to grow his first wheat. In 1835 Charles Darwin visited New Zealand on the H.M.S. *Beagle* and commented on the fine barley and wheat in the mission fields of Waimate North. It was harvested with sickle or scythe.

In the first days of settlement wheat helped the colony's economy. Johnny Jones of Waikouaiti supplied wheat in 1848 to the first settlers in Otago, Dillon did the same in Nelson, and Australians and Maoris competed to keep down the price of wheat in Auckland. By the eighteen-seventies the Canterbury Plains included good areas of wheat and in 1883 grain was the second most important export. After the introduction of refrigeration it took an inferior place, and today New Zealand has to import some of her wheat.

PLATE 37
Wheat ready for harvest at Kingsdown near Timaru.

THE spirit of man can soar freely in the Mackenzie Country, where one direction can give a view of forty miles of tussocks and another of Mount Cook, 12,349 feet, and some of its satellites. Summer is hot and winter is severe in this country of highland farms where isolated homesteads and huts shelter sheepmen and musterers.

The level of Lake Tekapo has been raised as part of a storage scheme for hydro-electric power development that culminates in the giant earth dam built down the Waitaki gorges at Benmore.

Lake Tekapo is always an impressive sight for travellers on the back-country route through South Canterbury and Otago. From Timaru over Burkes Pass, Tekapo is the first in a chain of eight long lakes of glacial origin, all of them set amongst mountains.

Tekapo is one of New Zealand's larger lakes, having a length of some fifteen miles and an area of around thirty-two square miles. This view of the lake does not show the very head, where the Godley River flows swiftly from glacier sources at the Main Divide past the high-country sheeprun of Lilybank. It shows the mountains of the Godley Peaks sheeprun, where men and dogs work hard mustering sheep, whose fine wool gives both pride and material prosperity to New Zealand. Problems of erosion exist in this country; excessive grazing and burning must be avoided if the steep pasture slopes are to remain stable.

Gliding clubs have annual meets here in the Mackenzie Country, and updraughts made by the nor'-west wind have enabled pilots to achieve amazing and record heights.

PLATE 38
Lake Tekapo from the road to Lake Alexandrina.

PINK foxgloves on flood-prone riverbed; ancient moraines covered by subalpine scrub; implication of mist on the right; arrival of mist on the left; and Sefton behind. There are no beg pardons about Sefton, 10,359 feet; its flanks climb straight up from the valley floor and dominate the sky.

This wall of broken icefalls, relieved, if that is the ironic word, by a few faces and ribs of loose greywacke rock, is one of the sights of the Southern Alps, accessible to all and climbed by few. The Footstool, 9,073 feet, is on the right, directly above the patch of mist. The bumpy ridge between The Footstool and Mount Sefton forms part of the Main Divide.

The snowfields on the other side of Mount Sefton can be reached by aircraft fitted with skis, but even before mountaineering degenerated to such tricks (tourists are another matter), the Westland route to the peak was not accounted as difficult. Much more hazardous is the traditional climb of the east face, here shown in full splendour, all of it in Canterbury, all of it alive with depth of crevasses and menace of avalanche.

To the right of the peak is a near-vertical face very near, if not actually the scene of, a dramatic escape from disaster by the men who made the first ascent of Mount Sefton in 1895. The English climber E. A. Fitz-Gerald and his guide Zurbriggen were on the ridge. Here are Fitz-Gerald's words: "... a large boulder that I touched with my right hand gave way with a great crash and fell, striking my chest ... The falling boulder hurled me down head foremost, and I fell about eight feet, turning a complete somersault in the air ... I struck against the side of the mountain with great force ...

"I was just contemplating how I should feel dashing down the 6,000 feet below, and wondering vaguely how many times I should strike the rocks on the way ... I was now swinging in the air like a pendulum, with my back to the mountain, scarcely touching the rock face."

PLATE 39
Mount Sefton, and The Footstool
from near The Hermitage.

And high lifted up to the north, the mountains,
the mighty, the white ones
rising sheer from the cloudy sea, light-crowned,
established.

THESE lines by Mary Ursula Bethell may have been written for the Kaikoura Ranges, but they apply well to the central Mount Cook region, a National Park since 1953.

Clouds that billowed across Westland from the Tasman Sea have, on meeting the Main Divide, dispersed to leave the Canterbury side clear.

The aircraft from which the photograph was taken has flown up the Dobson River from Lake Ohau and banked at the head of the valley, just short of the Barron Saddle. Beyond the saddle lies the valley of the Mueller Glacier, its trough crenellated by a striking shadow. (To the right of the shadow is the modest Sealy Range, on the other side of which, and well beyond our camera's eye, stands The Hermitage hotel.)

A similar shadow marks the moraine of the Hooker Valley beyond, the Hooker that leads directly to the base of Cook itself. On the extreme right another moraine and glacier valley, the Murchison, leads back to the Divide.

So much for the valleys; now for the peaks. In the centre rises Cook, its three peaks—the highest 12,349 feet—linked by a ridge that is above all else in this mountainous land.

To the immediate left of Cook and beyond is a cluster of jostling mountains, each hiding part of his neighbour in rather an abrupt way: Hicks (St Davids Dome), Tasman, Dampier. To the left again the shadowed peak of Sefton mounts the sky above the clouds and obscures in part the snowy, distant cone of La Perouse. The ridge of rock and ice in left centre links Burns (left), jagged Vampire, and sunlit Bannie, whose snowfall is bisected by shadow.

Down to the right from Cook, in production line pattern, fall the lesser peaks and ridges of the Mount Cook Range. Beyond are the snowfalls of the upper Tasman Valley and the peaks of the Minarets and Elie de Beaumont. The jumble of rocky peaks and spurs is the Malte Brun Range.

All these peaks have now been climbed, all these passes crossed. There remain a few unclimbed face routes of some hazard. There remain the old ways to accept or reject, the new ways if men can find them. Will his machine-ridden existence engulf him so that in the future he will climb merely by helicopter or alpine hovercraft? Or will men continue to find reward in the struggle against their own, and the mountains', weaknesses?

PLATE 40
Aerial view of the high peaks of
the Mount Cook National Park.

THE main highway is sturdy and wide between Christchurch and Dunedin. Many sections, **such as** this one between Oamaru and Herbert, give sidelong glances at snowy ranges forefronted by undulating hills. Farm buildings glisten in their shelter belts. Forage crops are greener than neighbouring grass. The land looks settled and productive.

Recurrent floods have been part of Maheno's story and are implicit in the name, which means "island". In the Kakanui Mountains, in the background, rises the Kakanui River which flows by the old settlement and which has, in the past, surrounded it.

The road and railway join the coast at Hampden further to the south, and from there to Dunedin they skirt high bluffs and fine bays.

About 1880 New Zealand faced a reduced output of gold and low prices for wool and tallow. There was a surplus of stock in New Zealand and a shortage of meat in England where her markets lay. The invention of refrigeration for the preserving of meat saved the economic life of New Zealand and increased the standard of living of her farmers. The export of frozen meat, and later of butter and cheese, became larger and more lucrative than wheat.

The trial shipment of frozen meat on the sailing ship *Dunedin* in 1882 included carcasses of 140 sheep and 101 lambs from Maheno. Thus this district took its share in a great event in New Zealand farming history. The new methods enabled the farmer of small holdings to keep his place on pasture land.

PLATE 41
Stud farm pastures near Maheno, North Otago.

THERE are some places in New Zealand of such incredible beauty that it is difficult for a camera or a pen to give them vitality on a printed page. Lake Wanaka is such a place.

Distant mountains of rugged rock and perching glaciers contrast with closer ranges, where the marks of glaciation have rounded, carved, curved, and modelled tussock spurs and slopes to shapes that change in varying lights as though animated. Early morning and evening give surprises that awaken the artist in man or woman responsive to nature. Cloud patterns and variations of light and colour add to the fascination of land forms, and below all this, there is the lake itself, sometimes whipped to fury by sudden storms, sometimes calm with an innocence that would tempt a canoe far from shore.

This view shows part of a large and thriving holiday settlement. The Cardrona Valley in the distant centre is flanked on the left by the Pisa Range, and on the right by a spur to Mount Alpha. A road up the valley crosses the Crown Range to 3,676 feet and a steep descent to Queenstown.

The region has history comparable to its scenery: Maori legends of animals which made floating houses and murmuring noises; exploring pastoralists with flax rafts; gold prospectors and miners. Today the lake has all the amenities of good roads, shops, launch trips, a fish hatchery, excellent trout fishing, and spacious camping places.

Wanaka is a springboard for trampers and mountaineers wishing to traverse the Matukituki Valley towards Mount Aspiring, 9,957 feet, seen in splendour from Glendhu Bay. Launch parties can travel the length of the lake and some of them land and explore the Wilkin Valley, majestic in its isolation, a place of wide river flats and beech forest, musterers' huts, and snowy peaks.

PLATE 42

Lake Wanaka and township, Otago Central.

JUST as perfection of outline and mass make a little mountain comparable for beauty with a giant neighbour, so does the attraction of blue pool and rapid in a tributary act as foil for the might of a great and more turbulent river.

The Hawea River joins the Clutha at Albert Town some two miles below the outlet of Lake Wanaka, and is said to be the shortest river in New Zealand. There are rainbow trout for anglers, some of the river banks are accessible, and picnic grounds are at many bends. The water is clear, a reminder of its source from glacier and snow. The sheep country on the skylines leads down to stately poplar trees and sheltered homesteads.

If Lake Wanaka has been spared despoliation by progress in the form of hydro-electric power schemes, Lake Hawea, mother of the Hawea River, has endured progress. Its level has been raised; drowned trees and flats testify to its suffering. In another way, progress has given some compensation; the new transalpine road across the Haast Pass from Otago to South Westland skirts the western shore of Lake Hawea as far as The Neck, where it passes to the east shore of upper Lake Wanaka and so to the Makarora Valley. The road now links with South Westland and so to the Fox and Franz Josef Glaciers. Tourists are assured of a magnificent round trip.

What a contrast this will make. The eroded hills of Tarras and the tawny slopes of Hawea will change to the bushed bluffs of the Haast, the forest avenues of South Westland, the roar of breakers, the tang of the Tasman Sea, and the song of bellbirds and tuis as obbligato for passing voices.

PLATE 43
The Hawea River near its junction with the Clutha.

A SPELL on the track to Ben Lomond, 5,747 feet, gives an early winter scene, rich with the absence of haze. The low afternoon sun has spotlit the rocky ramparts of Queenstown and highlighted the rocky ramparts of the Remarkables, whose apex of Double Cone, 7,688 feet, rises in the centre, its height emphasised alike by snow and the bands of cloud below. Between the forested peninsulas the Frankton Arm of the lake takes the eye to the scars of glaciation on Peninsula Hill. The slopes of the Remarkables are on the other side gentler, and give climbers easy access to the final rock crests which are loose and tremulous to the touch.

The full Maori name of Wakatipu is said to Wakatipuwai-maori, the trough of a monster, but although there is no subterranean inhabitant the lake waters rise and fall in a regular cycle like slow breathing. Prosaically the level of the lake is 1,016 feet above that of the sea; its depth is 1,239 feet. Of early Pakeha history there is nothing prosaic. Adventurous runholders searching for sheep country used rafts of flax-sticks to reach Queenstown. Prospectors suffered winter snowstorms and hunger in their searches for alluvial gold. By 1863 Queenstown was a lively mining town, to the irritation of the sheepmen, and in its first seven months sent 191,825 ounces of gold to Dunedin on the gold escort.

Today Queenstown is assured of tourist traffic throughout the year. Rainbow and brown trout are there for the angler. The tramper and mountaineer can choose between interesting pass crossings from the Rees Valley to the Dart, the twin peaks of Mount Earnslaw, 9,308 feet, or trips up the Routeburn and the Greenstone.

In summer Queenstown's hotels and boardinghouses are crammed to their roofs, its motorcamps bulge at the fences. The lake steamer sets out on its regular round with crowded decks, and tourist launches dart, spin, and flurry. During winter the ski-fields at Coronet Peak attract gay, colourful crowds. Between seasons the town provides for those who like to take their holidays at more leisurely pace and avoid scenic indigestion. Lake Wakatipu is under no threat from power development and Queenstown can cope with a lot of people without fraying at the edges.

PLATE 44
Queenstown and the Remarkables from above Lake Wakatipu.

GOLD in the river, farms and orchards irrigated by the river, power from the river—that is the story of Roxburgh.

In the early days of Central Otago, goldminers from Australia brought new methods of sluicing and transport of water. As the claims became worked out, the water races served orchards and farms, more grass grew and more crops for winter feed. The land that flourished from gold flourished with fruit and stock. Today the harnessing of the mighty Clutha for power has given new vigour to New Zealand.

The mountain lakes of Hawea, Wakatipu, and Wanaka feed the Clutha with generous natural storage of water from snow and rain, and this water spins the generators of the Roxburgh power station, one of the largest in New Zealand.

This hydro station, a major construction project conceived in 1944 and built by the Ministry of Works, overseas and New Zealand firms, solved a power shortage twelve years later. Three million tons of concrete were mixed for the dam and powerhouse. The dam is 1,200 feet long, 200 feet wide at the base, and 250 feet high from the lowest point of excavation; behind it lies a lake twenty miles long and two and a quarter square miles in area.

Our picture shows the dam and spillway, the powerhouse seemingly dwarfed by the concrete mass above, and the surge and tumult of the outflow. Transmission lines connect into the South Island electricity network.

PLATE 45
The Roxburgh dam spans the Clutha River.

THIS view of shipping, city, and suburbs at the head of Otago Harbour also shows the forested town belt.

The air is clear and cool in this city of the south.

One contemporary observer of New Zealand life wrote that "you feel that the day that you crossed from Canterbury to Otago you moved from England to Scotland politically . . . that life is very real in Dunedin, and very earnest, and that getting on is one of its goals". The influence of Scottish founders is a strong one and the climate too encourages work.

The harbour entrance was not charted until 1826 when Captain Herd marked anchorages. When the settlers for the Free Church colony arrived in March 1848 they applied their dogged energies to the pioneering skills with which they were endowed. Good sheep country in the interior gave a solid basis for prosperity and the gold rushes of the sixties drew to Otago men as hardy and as adventurous as the original settlers.

Leaders of the province stood by their church and worked hard for good education for their children. They founded the first university, where today a medical school is pre-eminent.

The kniphofias in the foreground, growing in the grounds of St Joseph's home for children, add gaiety to the harbour scene.

PLATE 46
The city of Dunedin from Waverley.

YOU do not need to view a whole lake to appreciate its beauty. Shaped by the constricted floor of the valley, calm water set in calm beech forest, Lake Fergus is one of the unhidden gems of Fiordland.

Lakes Gunn, Fergus, and Lochie lie close together, in descending order of size, at the head of the Eglinton Valley. Between and past them swings the road from Lake Te Anau, past the Divide, into the upper Hollyford Valley and so to the Homer Tunnel and Milford Sound.

Within a mile of our photographer's vantage point, looking south across Lake Fergus, three strong rivers rise—and flow north, south, and east to the sea. Lake Fergus itself is the northernmost source of the Eglinton, which feeds Lake Te Anau and thus the Waiau draining south. Northwards runs the Hollyford, a tearing, tossing river, and eastwards the Greenstone, grown from a lake like Fergus, empties into Lake Wakatipu and thence to the mighty Clutha.

Lake Fergus was first seen from the mountains to the east in 1861 by exploring sheepmen, D. McKellar and G. Gunn. Two years later the exploring goldminer, P. Q. Caples, discovered and named the magnificent Hollyford Valley, which he followed to the sea at Martins Bay.

The mountain ridge in the background is the northern outpost of the Livingstone Range, which overlooks the road from Te Anau as it follows the lake shore and the sweeping bends of the Eglinton River.

PLATE 47

Lake Fergus on the road from the Eglinton Valley to the Hollyford Valley.

SINBAD Gully to the left of Mitre Peak, 5,560 feet, the Narrows dead centre; and the steep shaft of the Stirling Valley overshadowed by The Lion; these are some of the great names in Milford Sound.

The sound receives some 300 inches of rain in a year from mist, shower, deluge, sleet, and snow, and when it rains the precipices are alive with waterfalls of dashing foam. The sound has by contrast its calm days, as this one, when the visitor can be told of glaciers that carved hanging valleys, of Maori quests for greenstone, of near-extinct birds, one of which, the kakapo, was re-discovered in 1961 in the Tutoko Valley.

Captain J. L. Stokes, of H.M.S. *Acheron*, who surveyed these cliffs, coasts, and waters in 1851 credited a Welsh whaler with naming Milford after the Haven in Wales, and described Milford Sound as "the most remarkable harbour yet visited by the *Acheron* in New Zealand". Donald Sutherland, a wanderer from Scotland, sailor, prospector, soldier, and sealer, anchored at Milford and settled there, first as hermit, then as prospector for greenstone and asbestos, and explorer who discovered the Sutherland Falls, 1,904 feet high. He married, ran an accommodation house, and died here at eighty-four years.

The sound is also known for the Milford Track from Lake Te Anau, for the road that passes through the Homer Tunnel, for its sandflies, for its modern hotel, for its visits by world cruise-ships, and for its daring service by light aircraft. Mountaineers acknowledge its challenges, especially that of Mitre Peak, first climbed by J. R. Dennistoun some fifty years ago. Sutherland did not believe that Dennistoun had reached the summit, but a party making the second ascent found the handkerchief that Dennistoun had left in a cairn. As part of the Fiordland National Park Milford Sound is controlled by a board responsible to the National Parks Authority of New Zealand.

PLATE 48
Mitre Peak and The Lion reflected in Milford Sound.

FEATHERY ferns, clearing mists of the morning, a promise of wind in the rat's-tail sky, mottled snow and steep bluffs above a hanging valley, a wide grassy river flat, beech trees in silhouette—this is the fringe of Fiordland.

Almost three million acres are contained by the boundaries of Fiordland National Park, and one of its mysteries is recorded in the name of the highest of the Earl Mountains, Mt Ngatimamoe. Popularly known as "the lost tribe of Fiordland", the Ngati-Mamoe people were defeated in tribal battles in the latter half of the eighteenth century, so tradition runs, and some of the survivors escaped across Lake Te Anau into forbidding country. Their last refuge is believed to have been the northern sounds directly west of the mountains in our picture and their last pathetic traces were found almost a century later.

It is a mistake to scurry through to Milford Sound from Lake Te Anau without leaving time to boil the billy for tea or to contemplate scenes such as this at leisure. Not far from here is a motel at Cascade Creek, where motorists can get accommodation and meals. Many New Zealanders are used to fending for themselves on holiday, with equipment ranging from canopied caravans to the lightweight gear of hardier and younger folk, who are equally content with pup tents, sleeping bags, and battered billies.

The Eglinton Valley offers good water for trout fishing and there are herds of red deer with the chance of a trophy head.

PLATE 49

The Earl Mountains, west of the Eglinton Valley.

DEPTH of 1,455 feet; height above sea-level, 599 feet; 59 square miles in area; 18 miles in length—these statistics cannot measure the perfection of Manapouri.

Fortunately modern colour photography can show, as in this view, the dignity of old beech trees and the grace of young ones, the barrier of the distant Cathedral Peaks and the changing patterns of lake surface broken by promontories. The lakes of Manapouri and Te Anau both have the characteristics of fiords, with deep arms fed by mountain rivers and thick bush. Heavy rainfall feeds the lakes and gives succour to the bush and plants. Glaciation has carved open, hanging valleys winter snowfall covers the summit ranges to melt in spring.

This is primeval New Zealand, where rare birds exist, where moose, wapiti, and deer forage in forest and on grassline, and where road and water access give countless travellers the thrill of walking, hunting, camping, and climbing.

There are two Maori versions for the name of the lake: the original Moturau meaning "many islands" and the longer Manawa-popore shortened to Manapouri meaning, so it is said, "Lake of the Sorrowing Heart". The fate of Manapouri makes "Sorrowing Heart" prophetic, because the New Zealand Government is raising the level of Manapouri to that of Te Anau as a storage area for a hydro-electric scheme at the head of Doubtful Sound.

There is considerable concern at the possible scenery damage resulting from the hydro scheme and there is a grave responsibility on the engineers and planners to retain for posterity the essential features of what has been described as "the loveliest lake in New Zealand".

PLATE 50
Above the outlet of Lake Manapouri.

"GREEN shall grow the grasses in the hard won field" was written by a young New Zealand farmer who died in World War II. The quotation recalls the lines by the Auckland poet, A. R. D. Fairburn

    . . . touch of soil and wind and rock
        frost and flower and water . . . .

The scene is south of Dipton on the main road between Lumsden and Winton, on the banks of the Oreti River, and under a Southland sky.

A New Zealand Thoreau once described Southlanders as "the people in New Zealand who live nearest to the Bible, and nearest to the soil". He also observed that Southland farmers "work longer hours than any other industry in the Dominion, and longer than any group in their own industry". It is true that pioneering habits of thrift and toil have lasted long in Southland, which is appropriate for country where the twilight gives hours that further north are enmeshed in darkness.

The Taringatura Hills are blue in the distance; clearly, the hills mapped as "Break my neck" and "Raggedy" are not visible. The house in shadow and the barn to the left of the cabbage trees are old. The district has been farmed for a full hundred years.

This is the famous fat-lamb country of Southland, where the sustained growth of the pastures is supplemented in winter by feed crops, and lambing percentages in spring are high. Many a British Sunday joint of "prime Canterbury lamb", has come from the Romney breeding ewes and Southdown rams of the plains beside the Oreti River.

PLATE 51
Pastoral country between Lumsden and Winton, Southland.

THE pilgrim trail of the colour camera ends for this volume on the southern coast of the South Island.

A traverse of both islands has shown the variations, the extreme contrasts, the merging of forest to farmland, and the transition from the headwaters of rivers to the coastal cliffs that border beaches. Harbours, plains, lakes, cities, and settlements have taken their place in a cross-section of New Zealand. Maori legend and Pakeha history have outcropped in the names: peaks have soared and stock has grazed.

New Zealand is for its size well-endowed with national parks, bush and scenic reserves, wild-life sanctuaries and re-fuges, offshore islands protected by law, and open spaces where families can stretch in the sun. Here, near the mouth of the Mataura, Maori warfare reached bitter conclusions. The accounts are controversial, but scenes of ancient slaughter are now a peaceful reserve.

The setting sun has given gold to Foveaux Strait, where Stewart Island, Rakiura—"The Island of the Glowing Sky" of the Maoris, lies by implication, but not by sight.

Thus a long twilight closes on southernmost New Zealand and our journey ends. Close the book with a Maori farewell: *E noho ra*—and hear the reply: *Haere ra!*

PLATE 52

Sunset at the Mataura River Estuary, Fortrose, Southland.

ACKNOWLEDGMENTS

In his research for the text, John Pascoe received willing help from the chief librarian and staff of the Alexander Turnbull Library, Wellington, especially Misses Iris Park and Elspeth Hill, and Mrs Gillian Ryan. He was also assisted by the staff of the National Archives and the General Assembly Library, Wellington.

Quotations in this book from the works of New Zealand poets are gratefully acknowledged to:

PENGUIN BOOKS. "Conversation in the Bush" and "Elements" both by A.R.D. Fairburn; "The Long Harbour "and "Southerly Sunday", both by Mary Ursula Bethell; all from *The Penguin Book of New Zealand Verse.*

WHITCOMBE & TOMBS LIMITED. "Sunset" and "The Farming Nation" both by Eileen Duggan; and "Harvesting Wheat" by F. H Woods; all from *New Zealand Farm and Station Verse.*